IMAGES
of America

FORT LEWIS

The 91st Infantry Division Monument commemorates the service of the "Wild West Division" which trained at Camp Lewis in World War I. The division was comprised of soldiers from the western United States and earned a reputation for bravery during the Meuse-Argonne Offensive in France in 1918. The statue was designed by Avard Fairbanks and dedicated by the 91st Division Veterans Association in 1930.

IMAGES
of America

FORT LEWIS

Alan H. Archambault

ARCADIA
PUBLISHING

Published by Arcadia Publishing
Charleston SC, Chicago IL, Portsmouth NH, San Francisco CA

Printed in the United States of America

Library of Congress Catalog Card Number: 2001098148

For all general information contact Arcadia Publishing at:
Telephone 843-853-2070
Fax 843-853-0044
E-Mail sales@arcadiapublishing.com
For customer service and orders:
Toll-Free 1-888-313-2665

Visit us on the Internet at www.arcadiapublishing.com

The Pacific Northwest is a region of great natural beauty and abundant wildlife. This vintage photograph captures both with a military theme. A local elk finds himself in the midst of a formation of infantrymen from Camp Lewis, c. 1918. Mount Rainier is visible in the distance.

CONTENTS

A color guard of a regiment assigned to the 3rd Infantry Division passes in review, 1937. Military pomp and circumstance has been a vital part of Fort Lewis' history since 1917.

INTRODUCTION

The United States Army has played a significant role in the exploration, settlement, and defense of the Pacific Northwest. In 1804, President Thomas Jefferson sent a trusted Army officer, Captain Meriwether Lewis, on an expedition with Captain William Clark to travel overland to the Pacific Coast. The military organization formed for the expedition was named the "Corps of Northwest Discovery." Most of its personnel were volunteers from the U.S. Army. These adventurers were the first American soldiers to serve in the Pacific Northwest. In addition to all the information that the expedition brought back to President Jefferson, the journey gave the United States the opportunity to claim the region for its own.

As American settlers began to arrive in the Puget Sound region in the mid-1800s, the United States Army was required to provide soldiers to protect American lives and interests. The Army, in essence, served as a police force, bringing law and order to the frontier. In 1849, the Army established Fort Steilacoom to provide a safe haven for American citizens, and to serve as a symbol of United States authority in the Washington Territory.

Beginning in 1904, the U.S. Army and the Washington National Guard held maneuvers at American Lake, Washington. These maneuvers were important as they introduced the military leaders to the advantages of locating an army post in the Puget Sound area. In 1916, the Army began to seriously consider locating a major installation in the vicinity of the American Lake maneuvers. A group of Tacoma businessmen formed a committee to promote the idea with both the military authorities and the citizens of Pierce County, in which the area was located. Eventually, the committee offered to donate 140 square miles of land to the Army if a permanent military installation was established. The proposal went to President Woodrow Wilson, who added his endorsement. Congress voted its approval of the plan on August 29, 1916.

The proposal to purchase the land and donate it to the Army was then presented to the voters of Piece County. On January 6, 1917, 86 percent of the Pierce County Electorate voted to bond themselves for 20 years for $2,000,000 to purchase 70,000 acres of land. This land would then be donated to the Federal government for use as an Army post. In April 1917, before all the land was legally acquired, the United States entered World War I. In order to expedite the building of the post, arrangements were made with the landowners to "borrow" the land until the negotiations were completed. It was not until November 1919 that title to the land was officially transferred from the citizens of Pierce County to the United States government. It is believed that Camp Lewis was the only Army installation created by the outright gift of land from the citizens of a county. However, one provision in the contract stated that if the land was not maintained by the government for the uses named, title to the land would revert back to the citizens of Pierce County.

Construction of the camp began on July 5, 1917. Originally known as Camp American Lake, the post was officially named Camp Lewis, in honor of Meriwether Lewis, on July 18, 1917. Ultimately, Camp Lewis was constructed in the shortest time and at the lowest cost of any army camp built during World War I. At the original cost of $7,000,723.51, 1,757 buildings and 422 other structures were erected in 90 days. The first recruits arrived to begin training on September 5, 1917. By December over 37,000 soldiers occupied the camp. The 91st Division, which was comprised primarily of men from the western states, was the first unit to train at Camp Lewis. Known as the "Wild West Division," the unit left for France in June 1918 and served gallantly in several campaigns. The 13th Division was organized at Camp Lewis following the departure of the 91st Division. However, the war ended before the 13th Division deployed overseas.

With the end of the "Great War" the nation turned its back on the military and Army appropriations were sharply reduced. Camp Lewis quickly changed from a bustling military post to a neglected "ghost town." The citizens of Pierce County reminded the United States Government of its contract, which they had made in good faith, and threatened to take the land back. As a result, when congress passed a 10-year building plan to revitalize selected Army posts, Camp Lewis was at the top of the list. Camp Lewis was therefore officially designated a fort on September 30, 1927. Construction soon began on the permanent brick barracks and military quarters which still grace Fort Lewis today.

As the clouds of war engulfed Europe and Asia in the late 1930s, military activity at Fort Lewis increased dramatically. The post population grew from 5,000 to 37,000 troops between May 1939 and March 1941. Initially, there was not enough barracks to house the troops and many lived in tent cities. To ease the situation, a complex of wood barracks was built on North Fort Lewis between 1940–1941. Following the attack on Pearl Harbor, Fort Lewis became a center for military defense of the Pacific Northwest. Soon units were training for overseas service. During the course of the war, the 3rd, 33rd, 40th, 41st, 44th, and 96th Infantry Divisions trained at Fort Lewis. In addition, many smaller units passed through the post. In 1943, a prisoner of war camp was established on Fort Lewis, housing primarily captured German soldiers. Camp Lewis was designated an Army Service Forces Training Center in 1944. The post then focused on the training of Army engineers and medical personnel.

At the end of World War II, Fort Lewis was recognized as one of the Army's premier posts. The 2nd Infantry Division was headquartered on Fort Lewis from 1947 to 1950. When the Korean War erupted in 1950, the Second Infantry Division became the first U.S. based division to deploy to combat. The post then concentrated on training and deploying troops to Korea. Following the end of the Korean War, Fort Lewis became the home of the 4th Infantry Division, nicknamed the "Famous Fourth." With the escalation of the war in Vietnam, the 4th Division deployed to Southeast Asia in 1966. Fort Lewis then became an Army Training Center for basic and advanced infantry training. A personnel center for processing soldiers to and from assignments in the Pacific was also established. By the end of the Vietnam War, over $2^1/_2$ million soldiers had been processed through the post and 300,000 had trained here.

In 1972, following service in Vietnam, the 9th Infantry Division was reactivated at Fort Lewis. The division eventually was designated "motorized" and served as an experimental force, testing new vehicles, weapons, and doctrine. The headquarters of I Corps was reactivated at Fort Lewis in 1981. Presently, I Corps serves on Fort Lewis as a power projection platform for the Pacific Region. During Operation Desert Storm, the I Corps and Fort Lewis commander, Lt. Gen. Calvin A.H. Waller, was deployed to serve as deputy commander of American forces serving in the Persian Gulf.

Following Operation Desert Storm, the 9th Infantry Division was inactivated and Fort Lewis began to play an important role in the "Transformation of the Army." The 1st Brigade of the 25th Infantry Division and the 3rd Brigade of the 2nd Infantry Division were selected to spearhead a transformation to "combat brigade teams" that can deploy anywhere in the world in 96 hours.

From its beginnings as a cantonment in World War I, to the cutting edge military technology of the 21st century, Fort Lewis has been instrumental in the defense of American freedom. Millions of dedicated men and women have served on Fort Lewis as soldiers, family members, or civilian employees. The entire history of Fort Lewis is one of service, honor, and sacrifice. This collection of historic images was selected from the archives of the Fort Lewis Military Museum. Housed in the "Red Shield Inn," the museum continues to collect photographs, information, and artifacts associated with the heritage of Fort Lewis and the United States Army. Although this publication can only highlight a few of the many units that served and the activities that occurred on the post, it is hoped that it will in some small measure serve as a reminder of their selfless service to our nation.

One

THE ARMY IN EARLY WASHINGTON

Troopers bearing the national and regimental colors of the 9th U.S. Cavalry Regiment pass in review during the 1904 American Lake Maneuvers. The 9th and 10th Cavalry Regiments were composed of African-American volunteers and were popularly known as "Buffalo Soldiers." Both units participated in the 1904 Maneuvers.

Captain Meriwether Lewis was selected by President Thomas Jefferson to lead the Corps of Northwest Discovery on its epic journey to the Pacific Coast in 1804–1806. Lewis was a young and intelligent officer who shared his command with his Army comrade, William Clark. The Lewis and Clark Expedition was a pivotal event in the early history of the American west. Unfortunately, Meriwether Lewis died under mysterious circumstances several years after the expedition. Camp Lewis was named in his honor shortly after it was established in July 1917.

The Lewis and Clark expedition was remarkable in that most Native Americans welcomed, and even assisted, the members of the expedition throughout the journey. Both Lewis and Clark took great pains to foster cordial relations between the local Indians and the young American government. The only violent confrontation took place when some Indians tried to steal the expedition's horses. This woodcut engraving is from an early history of the expedition.

Fort Steilacoom was established near Puget Sound in 1849. The fort was located near a Hudson's Bay trading post named Fort Nisqually, perhaps to intimidate the British. The soldiers of Company M, 1st U.S. Artillery Regiment, first occupied the fort, followed later by companies from the 4th and 9th Infantry Regiments. During the Puget Sound Indian War of 1855–1856, Fort Steilacoom became a refuge for American settlers. Soldiers from Fort Steilacoom were also instrumental in protecting settlers from Indian attacks and projecting an American presence in the region. This photograph depicts the post shortly before it was closed in 1868. The buildings depicted were constructed *c.* 1858.

Lt. Col. Silas Casey of the 9th U.S. Infantry Regiment was one of the most prominent commanders of Fort Steilacoom. A graduate of the West Point Class of 1826, Casey saw active service against the Seminoles in Florida and in the Mexican-American War. Casey's wife and family served with him at Fort Steilacoom and provided a domestic touch of gentility to the rugged frontier post. His daughters also engaged the attention of young unmarried officers on post. During the Civil War, Casey attained the rank of major general although his field service was limited due to his age. This photograph depicts him as a brigadier general.

Two soldiers of the Washington Militia are depicted in a studio photograph taken *c.* 1898. After Washington achieved statehood in 1889, an effort was made to improve the state's military forces. During the Spanish-American War period the 1st Washington Volunteer Infantry served in the Philippines where they served to suppress insurgents.

PREPARATIONS BEING MADE FOR MANEUVERS AT AMERICAN LAKE

IMPRESSIONS OF A TENDERFOOT WITH THE EIGHTH BATTERY

AN IDEAL COOK TENT

CAPT KENLEY OF THE EIGHTH FIELD ARTILLERY

CAPT. LAWTON AS WORKING OVERTIME

WITH THE SOLDIERS IN THE VICINITY OF AMERICAN LAKE.

The 1904 Military Maneuvers held at American Lake marked a turning point in the military history of Washington. Two armies, the blue army and brown army, made up of regular U.S. Army units and of local militia organizations, battled it out in a series of war games around American Lake. Regular Army officers engaged in the maneuvers came to see the area as a potential military training ground for large-scale operations. Similar maneuvers where held in 1906, 1908, 1910, and 1912. This cartoon reflects the public's interest in the maneuvers.

Three medical corpsmen administer aid to a mock casualty during the American Lake Maneuvers in 1904. The rural atmosphere of the American Lake area can be seen in the snake rail fence and lush vegetation.

In this photograph of the 1904 Maneuvers, it can be seen that the U.S. Army was still a horse-drawn organization. Thousand of horses and mules participated in the maneuvers. They were used by the artillery, quartermaster, and of course, cavalry units.

Foot soldiers were still the backbone of the army in 1904. This group depicts an infantry regiment from Washington marching in battle formation. Both cotton khaki and blue wool uniforms were worn by American troops during this time period.

A group of soldiers serving with Company A, Signal Corps, National Guard of Washington, are depicted at the mess table during the 1910 American Lake Maneuvers. By this date, olive drab uniforms were worn by both state and regular U.S. Army troops.

This group of young Washington National Guardsmen with mess plates and cups was photographed in 1912 during the maneuvers.

CAMP LEWIS

TACOMA WN.

The cover of a Camp Lewis booklet from 1917 depicts the new Cantonment with Mount Rainier looming in the distance. Depending on atmospheric conditions, the mountain can seem many miles away or right at the edge of the post. Of course, many days the mountain cannot be seen at all due to cloud cover.

Two

The Establishment of Camp Lewis

This is a familiar view to many doughboys: the cantonment and Mount Rainier.

Lt. Col. David L. Stone was the driving force behind the construction of Camp Lewis. Stone arrived in May 1917, as a captain in the Quartermaster Corps, to supervise the construction of the camp. Through his diligence and organizational abilities, Camp Lewis was constructed in the shortest period of time and at the lowest cost of any Army camp built in World War I. Promoted several times during the war, Stone returned to command Fort Lewis in 1936 as a major general.

The dedicated and capable staff of Lt. Col. David Stone pose in this photograph, c. 1918.

Above is a view of the construction of Camp Lewis in the summer of 1917. Ten thousand men built the entire camp in 90 days.

Barracks are under construction in this photograph of Camp Lewis. Erected were 1,757 buildings, along with 422 other structures between July and September 1917.

A 1917 pamphlet and map shows the location of Camp Lewis. Many of these souvenir publications were purchased by soldiers to send to loved ones and friends.

Published in 1917 was a "Birdseye View Camp Lewis." The layout of the camp and the

Corporal Herman W. Hauck was the first recruit to arrive at Camp Lewis on September 1, 1917. He was the first of 60,000 men to train at Camp Lewis in World War I.

importance of the roads and rail lines can be seen in this picture map.

Maj. Gen. Henry A. Greene was the first commander of Camp Lewis and the 91st Division. He was a Class of 1879 West Point graduate, and a veteran of campaigns in Cuba and the Philippine Islands. Although he was a capable commander, he was thought to be too old to lead the 91st Division to France and was therefore left behind at Camp Lewis.

This view of Camp Lewis shows the relationship of the railroad tracks, the warehouses, and the numerous barracks.

Boys will be boys and the soldiers of Camp Lewis loved to pose for humorous photographs. For many men their "Army Days" became the high point of their lives.

The regimental colors of the various units of the 91st Division are massed in this impressive ceremony held at Camp Lewis. Activities like this instilled a sense of pride in the men training at Camp Lewis.

The doughboys who trained at Camp Lewis were primarily from the cities, farms, ranches, and towns of the western states. Generally, they were young and healthy and soon became rugged and dependable soldiers.

Standing in line has always been a distinct feature of military life. Here, a group of Camp Lewis doughboys practice the art. Hopefully, they are standing in line to see a motion picture in the building rather than getting inoculations.

Soldiering was a new experience for most of the recruits and as they learned to be fighting men, they often liked to have their photographs taken in warlike poses. This doughboy demonstrates a bayonet thrust for the folks back home. He is armed with a Model 1917 Enfield rifle and bayonet. His campaign hat and canvas leggings are typical of recruits in stateside training. When soldiers arrived in France, steel helmets and spiral puttees were issued and would become the standard wear on the Western Front.

The soldiers of Camp Lewis had a good sense of humor and liked to poke fun at themselves and their comrades. This cartoon was drawn for the post newspaper by a soldier-artist in 1917.

Boxing was one of America's most popular male sports and weekly boxing matches were held on Camp Lewis during World War I. Boxing was held in high esteem by the military as a "manly art" and its skills and aggressiveness were considered a warlike virtue. This posed photograph was taken on Camp Lewis in 1917 and depicts members of Company F, 363rd Infantry Regiment.

Americans were very sentimental during the World War I period and many were dog lovers. Therefore, this cartoon reflected a popular sentiment. Actually, almost every unit at Camp Lewis had a mascot, usually a dog. An article written during the war addressed the fact that there were hundreds of dogs living with the soldiers at Camp Lewis.

"When a Feller Needs a Friend"

—Drawn by Briggs of the New York Tribune for Trench and Camp

Most soldiers were God-fearing, and this photograph depicts a church service held at the Hostess House in 1918. In addition to the soldiers there are also young visitors to the camp in attendance.

Church Service — Hostess House
Camp Lewis

When Camp Lewis was built in 1917, many service organizations were allowed to build facilities to serve the soldiers. The Young Women's Christian Association (YWCA) built a hostess house where soldiers could seek wholesome entertainment and a touch of home.

The American Red Cross hostess house on Camp Lewis was very popular with the troops. The building still stands on Fort Lewis and is now used as a family resource center.

Miss Vivian Gough was a young violinist from Tacoma who often came to Camp Lewis to play for the troops. She also corresponded with several of the soldiers who served in France and in 1991 she donated the letters to the Fort Lewis Museum.

A group of staff members, volunteers, visitors, and soldiers pose in front of the Red Cross Hostess House in 1918.

Many businesses catered to the military market provided by Camp Lewis. The Liberty Studio was one such enterprise.

The Red Shield Inn was built by the Salvation Army towards the end of World War I to augment their smaller facility, called the "hut," which had been built in 1917. The Inn provided rooms for visitors to the post as well as family members. In addition to lodging, the Inn offered a music room, a reading room, and a dining room. Major social functions were often held at the Inn. Today, the Red Shield Inn is the home of the Fort Lewis Military Museum.

The Main Gate of Fort Lewis has been a landmark of the post since it was built in 1917. The structure was built to resemble a pioneer blockhouse, used to protect settlers. The civilian workers who built the post donated the time and money required to erect the gate and then donated it to the camp.

A World War I view of the Main Gate often called "The Liberty Gate."

Miss Jenny Booth was Chief of Nurses at the post hospital at Camp Lewis during World War I. This was the first conflict where women played a major role in the medical care of the soldiers.

This humorous cartoon relates to a serious issue. The Spanish Flu epidemic of 1918 killed as many American soldiers as died in battle. Although Camp Lewis was not hit as hard by the flu as some posts, it was a major source of

Any Available Alibi

By LEE WISE
Headquarters Co.

BATTALION INFIRMARY

I KIN EAT WELL AN SLEEP FINE, BUT I DONT SEEM TO HAVE ANY DESIRE TO WORK- I THINK I GOT THAT 'SPANISH FLU' GUESS I CANT K.P. ANY MORE

SOUNDS LIKE MEXICAN BULL TO ME

The soldiers who trained at Camp Lewis underwent serious training based on the experiences of the Allied forces. Here a doughboy leaps with his rifle and bayonet under the watchful eye of an instructor.

A regimental parade at Camp Lewis was in order prior to the departure of the 91st Division. By the time the troops left Camp Lewis for France they were accomplished soldiers.

World War I was the first conflict in which airplanes played a major role. Here, one of the first DH-4 biplanes to land on Camp Lewis sits on a makeshift airfield.

With the construction of over 1,700 "temporary" wood buildings on Camp Lewis during World War I, fire was a constant threat. Therefore, Camp Lewis had its own fire department, complete with early "state of the art" fire trucks.

Horses and mules were still the main source of moving supplies during World War I, and Camp Lewis was home to a large re-mount station. In this photograph, troops training to pack horses and mules with supplies pose with their wooden horses.

Since many of the soldiers at Camp Lewis were cowboys, it was natural to have a rodeo. One of the largest rodeos ever held in the Pacific Northwest occurred on Camp Lewis in July 1918.

Miss Ethel Allen was the first Red Cross Nurse's Aid to serve at Camp Lewis. She was the daughter of Col. S.E. Allen, Commander of the North Pacific District of the Coast Artillery Corps based in Seattle.

Since many of the soldiers who trained at Camp Lewis hailed from neighboring states, certain days were set aside to recognize the most popular states represented by the soldiers. The YMCA and other charitable organizations that served the needs of the soldiers usually coordinated these activities. This photograph depicts Montana Day, which was held on July 23, 1918. The soldiers would usually listen to patriotic lectures and sing popular songs as well as play games and socialize with each other and visiting hometown representatives.

36

It was natural that "America's favorite pastime" would be popular with the recruits at Camp Lewis. The military authorities realized the benefits of team sports in promoting physical exercise and teamwork. Most of the units on Camp Lewis had baseball teams that would play each other as well as local civilian organizations.

Football was growing in popularity during World War I and most units on Camp Lewis fielded enthusiastic teams. Since most of the college "All American" players were in the military in 1918, President Wilson allowed the Camp Lewis team to play a Marine team from Mare Island, California, in the Rose Ball. The game was played in Pasadena on New Year's Day, 1918, and the Marines won 19-7.

Mascots have played an important role in promoting high morale and the pride of soldiers in their units. Although dogs were the most common forms of mascot, some units took pride in having exotic pets. An example is this bear cub which was the mascot of the 16th Field Artillery which trained on Camp Lewis during World War I. This photograph was taken in 1918.

Enlisted men's clubs offered the soldiers a place to read, write letters, and play games. This photograph illustrates a typical club on Camp Lewis during World War I.

In spite of past injustices, Native Americans have proudly served in the Armed Forces of the United States in times of war and peace. During the First World War, one of our nation's Native American heroes was Squa-De-Lah, also known as Eli George. He was a member of the Nisqually Indian tribe and a descendent of Chief Sealth and Chief Kitsap. Following American's entry into World War I, Squa-De-Lah trained at Camp Lewis prior to deployment to France. Sadly, on Christmas Day 1917, he became the first Native American soldier to die on the Western Front.

Moe McKinley from Skamakawa, Washington was another Camp Lewis soldier to die in France. He served with Company B, 361st Infantry, 91st Division, and was killed in action in 1918.

By the end of World War I, the Main Gate of Camp Lewis had become an enduring symbol of the post. The worker's who built Camp Lewis donated approximately $4,000 for the materials to build the structure out of fieldstones and squared logs. Many soldiers and visitors to the post used the main gate as the backdrop for their photographs.

From 1917 through 1956 all traffic arriving at Camp or Fort Lewis passed through the main gate. In this World War I view, several military policemen stand guard.

Three

FROM CAMP TO FORT

Following the aviation pioneer Charles Lindbergh's celebrated transcontinental flight, he made a promotional tour of installations around the United States. Here he is seen receiving a salute from Battery D of the 10th Field Artillery on the parade ground at Fort Lewis. The construction of new barracks can be seen in the distance.

Boys, You Will Be Missed When You Are Gone
BY PHILIP LITTLE

CAMP LEWIS

THE BOYS HAVE GONE HOME

This cartoon reflects the state of Camp Lewis at the end of World War I. The little dog obviously misses his doughboy friends.

In order to keep the post alive, training continued on a limited scale. Often the soldiers were members of the National Guard or Reserve Officers Training Corps (ROTC). This photograph of unknown troops dates from the early 1920s.

Elements of the 4th Infantry Division served at Camp Lewis following World War I. This photograph depicts members of an infantry unit at Camp Lewis in 1919.

"A proud Papa:" Lieutenant Charles H. Swartz poses with his infant daughter, Isabelle, in 1922. Charles Swartz went on to become a brigadier general, and his daughter grew up to be a colonel in the Women's Army Corps. While serving on Camp Lewis, the Swartz family was quartered in the Red Shield Inn.

Due to 1920s budget constraints, an army truck serves as a school bus for Camp Lewis children.

The old and the new: in the years following World War I, most field artillery was still drawn by horses as depicted in this photograph. The cannons are the famous "French 75s".

The value of the Tank Corps was proven on the battlefields of the First World War. Therefore, following the conflict, the U.S. Army trained extensively with this new instrument of war. Originally, the tanks were used primarily in support of the infantry and were viewed as moving fortifications. This photograph was taken at Camp Lewis during the 1920s. The soldiers sit on a version of a French designed Renault FT-17 tank. This tank is "armed" with a dummy cannon, while others were equipped with machine guns or 37mm guns. At the time this photograph was taken few soldiers could have imagined the great armored divisions with powerful tanks that would emerge during the Second World War.

The 91st Division Monument was officially unveiled and dedicated on Memorial Day, 1930.

In the years following World War I, many of the cantonment's buildings constructed during the war were torn down. This included the amusement area known as Greene Park. This aerial view shows that the Red Shield Inn and the Salvation Army "Hut" are all that remain of the park's numerous structures. At the time of this photograph, Highway 99 still divides North Fort from the Main Post. The Main Gate is located towards the bottom left of the photograph and shows its original location in relationship to the Inn.

In 1921 the Salvation Army decided that it no longer wished to operate the Red Shield Inn and the building was sold to the Army on a "quit claim" deed for the cost of $1. The building was renamed the Camp Lewis Inn and continued to provide lodging for both visitors and officers assigned to the post. This photograph was taken in April 1937 and depicts Lieutenant Lewis D. Morgan, his wife Katherine, and his infant son, Thomas. They are posed in front of the Camp Lewis Inn, which was their home at that time. Thomas grew up to attend West Point and retired as a lieutenant colonel. He saw service with the Special Forces in Vietnam.

Above is a view of the Camp Lewis Inn. When the post was designated a fort in 1927, the name was changed to the Fort Lewis Inn. It kept this name until 1973 when the building became the home of the Fort Lewis Military Museum.

Were there Germans at Camp Lewis? No, these are extras and actors photographed during the filming of the motion picture, *The Patent Leather Kid*. The movie was filmed at Camp Lewis during the winter and spring of 1927. Many Camp Lewis soldiers with their equipment were "borrowed" for the battle scenes.

One of the highlights of the film was a scene where an American tank crashes into a French church. A mock French village was erected in the training area of Camp Lewis for the movie.

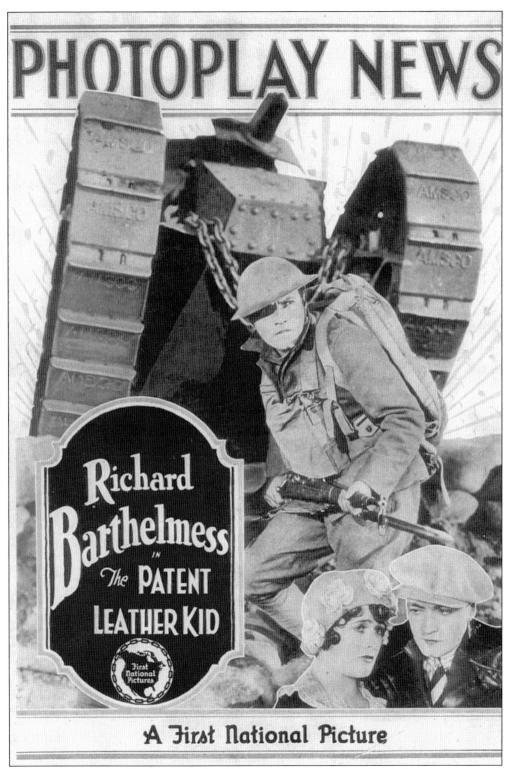

An advertisement for *The Patent Leather Kid* shows the star, Richard Barthelmess.

In spite of its brush with Hollywood fame, life at Camp Lewis remained austere by civilian standards as seen in this mess hall photograph.

Civilian Military Training Camps (CMTC) schooled young volunteers on the rudiments of military life. Many of the young men who participated in the CMTC later used the experience to obtain officer's commissions during the Second World War.

Throughout the 1920s and '30s mules continue to haul military equipment. Here a Washington National Guard water wagon is driven across Camp Lewis during a training exercise.

When Camp Lewis was designated Fort Lewis in 1927, a major building project soon began. The commanding officer's quarters were officially known to the Army as "Field Officer's Quarters, Type D." The home was completed on November 9, 1934, at the cost of $14,500. The home remains the residence of the Fort Lewis commander to this day.

Horse drawn field artillery appears in formation during the 1930s. Behind the unit the newly constructed brick barracks and motor vehicles can be seen.

This aerial view of Fort Lewis depicts the newly built officers' quarters in a military housing area known as "Broadmoor." The larger buildings to the right in the photograph are new brick barracks for the soldiers.

This photograph from 1940 shows the construction of the main post hospital complex. The other large buildings under construction are administrative offices, while the smaller buildings are family quarters for senior non-commissioned officers.

The regimental band of the 15th Infantry Regiment pose in front of the 91st Division Monument. The white cross belts, caps, and leggings are reflective of the military styles often seen in the pre-World War II "Old Army."

Four

BETWEEN THE WARS

A unit of 37mm anti-tank guns deploy near a Fort Lewis barracks area just prior to World War II. These cannons would see much use during the coming war.

An artillery unit trains with 75mm pack howitzers c. 1940. These cannons could be disassembled and packed on the mules standing in the background.

A ceremonial massing of the colors of the 3rd Infantry Division on Fort Lewis, c. 1938, reflects the build up of the forces on post at that time.

Members of the 115th Cavalry Regiment demonstrate their abilities in this 1940 photograph.

A group of soldiers serving in the 15th Infantry Regiment are "standing tall" after receiving awards in this 1938 photograph.

One of the highlights of the soldiers' day was mealtime, or "chow time," as it was often called. While training in the field, soldiers would line up with their mess tins to receive their rations from the unit cooks. Here a group of soldiers from the 10th Field Artillery pose for the camera while getting their chow. The photograph dates from 1940.

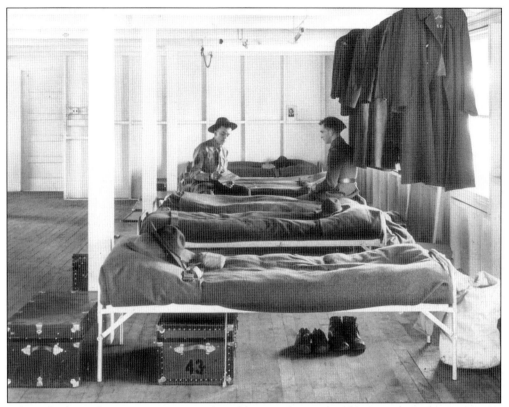

Life in the barracks was pretty spartan for soldiers in the pre-World War II army. However, the army was a good place to be for many young men during the years of the Great Depression.

The Civilian Conservation Corps (CCC) was begun in the Depression years to provide work for young Americans and to undertake many public works projects. Reserve Army officers were called to duty to lead the CCC camps that were organized on military examples. One such camp, located near Fort Lewis, was Camp Roy. It was commanded by Lt. Lewis D. Morgan, who appears in this photograph of a formation near the camp flagpole.

The 15th Infantry Regiment was a historic unit that returned from many years of duty in China and was posted to Fort Lewis. This photograph depicts members of the regiment on parade at Fort Lewis in 1938.

The M2, .50 caliber machine gun was a powerful and accurate weapon in the U.S. Army arsenal. Here, soldiers man an M2 while training on Fort Lewis in 1940.

Communications were an important aspect of army training, and these soldiers practice with radio equipment during the late 1930s.

This M2, .50 Caliber machine gun is manned by a unit mascot.

Sports were an important part of army life in the "Old Army." This photograph of the Fort Lewis basketball team dates from the late 1930s.

During a military review of the 3rd Division in early 1941, a unit of pack artillery and their mules pass the reviewing stand.

Life for officers was always a bit better than that of the average enlisted man. This officer sits by the fireplace in the lobby of the Fort Lewis Inn.

Barracks life for the enlisted men was simple but could be enjoyable with music provided by a radio or phonograph.

In the field, soldiers slept in two-man "pup" tents made up of two shelter halves. Each soldier carried one shelter half and then two men buttoned them together to form a small tent. This "gag" photo was the result of typical soldier humor.

During inspections soldiers would lay out all their equipment for inspection by sergeants and officers. This Fort Lewis photograph dates from 1941. The weapon in the foreground is a Model 1919, Browning air-cooled, .30 caliber, machine gun.

Lt. Col. Dwight D. Eisenhower served at Fort Lewis from November 1940 to June 1941. Much of his time was spent as chief of staff of the IX Army corps. He was known as being "amiable and efficient." These qualities would serve him well in his career as a general and U.S. president.

Reflective of the large build-up of the army prior to World War II, this photograph depicts soldiers watching a review of the Third Infantry Division on Fort Lewis in 1941.

Here is an impressive review of troops in front of the 91st Division Monument in 1941. The mounted troops are from the 115th Cavalry Regiment. A brutal war was just on the horizon for the soldiers in this historic photograph.

Five

WORLD WAR II

Fort Lewis soldiers march in an Army Day parade in downtown Tacoma in 1941.

In the first days of World War II, some Fort Lewis soldiers slept in tent cities due to lack of barracks rooms. This situation was soon remedied by the opening of the new wood barracks on North Fort Lewis.

After the attack on Pearl Harbor, many Fort Lewis troops were deployed around the Pacific Northwest to protect against enemy attack. This machine gun "nest" is typical of the defensive positions taken up by Fort Lewis troops.

The troops of the 115th Cavalry Regiment parade on Fort Lewis on the eve of war. The U.S. Horse Cavalry would be abolished in 1942.

New technology in warfare is reflected in these anti-aircraft guns being set up at Fort Lewis following the Japanese attack on Pearl Harbor in 1941.

Sergeant Joe Galli, noted as the oldest and ablest bugler in the United States Army, served in the 30th Infantry Regiment, 3rd Division, at Fort Lewis in 1941.

With the surge of patriotism stirred by the Japanese attack on Pearl Harbor on December 7, 1941, the recruiting offices on Fort Lewis were kept busy with eager volunteers. This photograph was taken by the Signal Corps detachment on Fort Lewis and was perhaps used to encourage other potential young recruits to enlist in Uncle Sam's Army.

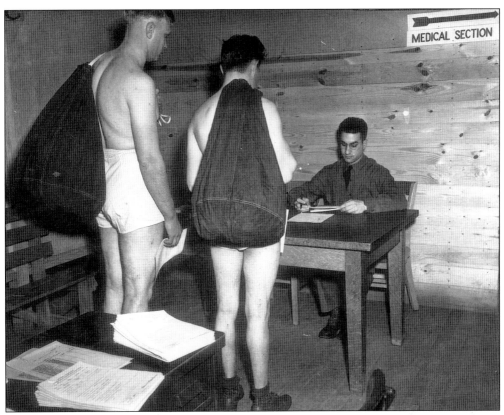

Tens of thousands of new recruits were processed through Fort Lewis during the Second World War. Two young trainees are depicted in this photograph. They patiently wait in their "skivvies" while an administration clerk processes the necessary paperwork. Both recruits carry their barracks bags, probably containing their civilian clothing, over their shoulders. The "civvies" were usually sent home by mail and the soldiers were only allowed to have military uniforms in their possession.

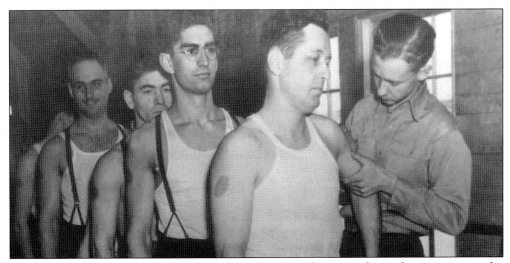

One of the ordeals of in-processing into the Army were the array of inoculations given to the new soldiers.

Another menace to the new recruits on Fort Lewis were the experienced sergeants who were willing and eager to point out a young soldier's shortcomings.

Soldier life during World War II is well illustrated in this photograph of a Fort Lewis barracks.

Battery "C" ★ 9th Field Artillery

This inspiring photograph of Battery C, 9th Field Artillery, appeared in a Fort Lewis news magazine named *The Sentinel* in 1941.

During World War II bugle calls were still an important part of the Army's daily routine. Several large megaphones were installed around Fort Lewis to assist the buglers in projecting the sound of their instruments to thousands of soldiers on post. This private first class is depicted blowing reveille to awaken the slumbering troops to a new day of activities. The bugler is armed with a pistol, perhaps to defend himself against irate soldiers who disliked being awakened so early. The photograph is dated 1943.

The Post Headquarters and the garrison flag are depicted in this World War II postcard. An observation balloon can also be seen in the distance.

"Old soldiers" managed to snooze whenever the opportunity arose as illustrated by this sergeant at rest in the field at Fort Lewis.

This observation balloon named "Minnie" belonged to the 3rd Balloon Company stationed at Fort Lewis in 1941.

The soldiers of the 144th Field Artillery pose with one of their 155mm guns during World War II. This particular cannon was nicknamed "Old Grizzly" by the troops.

A jeep driven by members of the headquarters staff, 15th Infantry Regiment, poses with its drivers in front of their unit headquarters. The unit motto was "Can Do", reflecting their service in China prior to the war. As part of the 3rd Infantry Division, the 15th Infantry left Fort Lewis in 1942 and served with distinction in the European Theater of Operations.

Non-commissioned officers have always formed the backbone of the army, and these veteran soldiers serving on Fort Lewis have 385 years of combined service. The soldiers, from left to right, are: (front row) Sgt. Charles V. West (30 years), M. Sgt. Frank B. Seahill (26 years), M. Sgt. Benjamin Cantrell (23 years), T. Sgt. Thomas Skrobut (28 years), and Sgt. Charles Donilitz (25 years); (second row) Staff Sgt. Herbert Evans (21 years), Tech. 5 Oscar Ressler (23 years), Pvt. Sam Williams (27 years), and Pvt. Emil Harer (27 years); (third row) T5g. James Cooney (23 years), Pvt. Joseph Kopec (29 years), T. Sgt. Robert Hotchkins (23 years), and T. Sgt. Frank Wihs (24 years); (top row) Staff Sgt. Richard Poole (25 years), Sgt. Lyman Price (31 years).

Practice makes perfect. This unit band marches down a dusty road on Fort Lewis during World War II.

Pictured is the Army's First "Barberette." Miss Gertrude Alto was the first woman barber to be employed by the U.S. Army. Miss Alto is depicted cutting the hair of Cpl. Donald "Red" Blanchard, while Pvts. Albert Carr, Harry Erath, and Jim Ball wait their turn.

"Everything in triplicate." The army has always produced a lot of paperwork, and during World War II many soldiers were assigned to administrative tasks. Although not as celebrated as the combat soldiers, these men also served with dedication and did their bit for the war effort.

During World War II training at Fort Lewis, a 3rd Infantry Division soldier receives dental care in the field.

One of the little "Blitz Buggies" of the 194th Tank Battalion stopped in almost full flight by the Sentinel camera man.

This action shot depicts a jeep, which some troops called a "blitz buggy," of the 194th Tank Battalion, training on Fort Lewis.

The chapel at Fort Lewis was a busy place during World War II, as many soldiers found love in wartime. This photograph depicts Lt. William L. Ramsden, judo instructor for the military police company, and his bride Kathryn Fry, passing under an arch of sub-machine guns.

The training at Fort Lewis paid off as units were highly trained by the time they left for overseas service. Here a unit passes in review on Fort Lewis in 1943.

SKI TROOPERS from FORT LEWIS at MOUNT RAINIER, WASHINGTON

One of the advantages of serving on Fort Lewis was the availability of the mountains for specialized training. A number of units sent soldiers to mountain training on Mount Rainier. On December 8, 1941, the Army activated its first official mountain unit. The 87th Mountain Infantry Battalion (later regiment) was organized at Fort Lewis and eventually formed the nucleus of the famous 10th Mountain Division.

With the construction of hundreds of "temporary" wood buildings during the World War II era, the members of the Fort Lewis Fire Department had a challenging job. Fire prevention and fire fighting became perfected as a serious profession during this time period. Both military personnel and civilian employees have faithfully served the post over the years. This photograph depicts a fire truck and crew posed in front of the Fort Lewis Fire Department headquarters.

The cadet nurse program gave valuable training to young women who went on to become military nurses. The hospital at Fort Lewis trained many cadet nurses during World War II. Typical of the young cadet nurses is Marion D. Sydenham, who went on to serve as an Army nurse.

The station hospital on Fort Lewis is depicted in this 1943 photograph.

This photograph depicts the activities of Army nurses at Madigan Army Hospital during World War II.

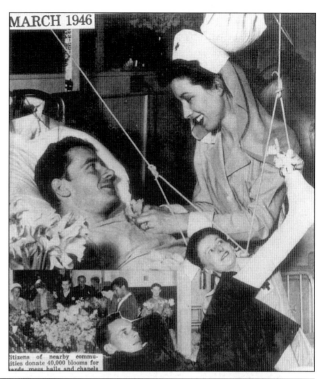

The need for increased hospital facilities at Fort Lewis during World War II led to the construction of a new $3 million addition to the post medical facilities. Construction began in 1943 and was completed in 1945. The new hospital was dedicated to Col. Patrick S. Madigan. The hospital complex had eight miles of corridors and hundreds of wards spread out throughout Fort Lewis.

In 1943, the first detachment of Women's Army Corps (WAC) personnel arrived on Fort Lewis. These women volunteered to serve their country to free up men for the battlefront. They were primarily engaged in clerical duties and became well known for their efficiency and devotion to duty. Fort Lewis soon became dependent on their abilities to provide support for all post functions. This photograph depicts the moment when the first WACs passed through the gates of Fort Lewis.

This 1944 ceremony was conducted to present Good Conduct Medals to members of the Women's Army Corps detachment serving on Fort Lewis.

A group of WACs pose at the train station in Tacoma as they await transportation to Fort Lewis in 1943.

Soldiers often staged shows for their comrades in arms. This scene was part of a show called "Sound Off." U.S. Army Pvt. Werner Klemperer portrays Adolph Hitler in a funny skit entitled "Pot O' Gold." Klemperer went on in show business to play Col. Klink on the *Hogan's Heroes* television show.

World Heavyweight Champion Joe Lewis visited Fort Lewis as a sergeant in the army. Here he is seen shaking hands with the post commander, Col. Max W. Sullivan. Cpl. Walter Smith, also known as Sugar Ray Robinson, also visited the post as part of a promotional tour.

Army bands also provided entertainment and inspiration to the troops. This World War II photograph depicts the 359th Army Service Force Band stationed at Fort Lewis.

This aerial view of Fort Lewis in the late 1940s reflects the permanent nature of the post. The post headquarters and Pershing Circle are in the foreground.

Six

THE KOREAN WAR ERA

A company of the 9th Infantry Regiment, 2nd Infantry Division passes in review in front of the regimental headquarters in 1950.

Several beauty contests were held to pick "Miss Second Division" in 1947. They were part of the ceremonies held to welcome the division to Fort Lewis. In this photograph, Native American Edward Kingbird, who often officiated at unit functions, poses with Miss Eileen Larson, Tacoma's Miss Second Division and Miss Marjorie Donnell, Olympia's Miss Second Division.

The 50th Infantry Scout Platoon of the 2nd Infantry Division was popular with both the soldiers and the public. They are depicted parading on Fort Lewis in 1947.

The soldiers of the 2nd Infantry Division trained hard on Fort Lewis between 1947 and 1950. When the Korean War began they were ready and able to deploy to combat.

Another unit that trained on Fort Lewis for duty in Korea was the Canadian Army Special Force. They arrived on Fort Lewis in October 1950 and underwent intensive combat training. The unit went on to serve with distinction in Korea.

Mountain and winter training continued to be conducted at Mount Rainier during the Korean War. In this photograph members of the 4th Regimental Combat Team learn to load a military type toboggan. These toboggans could be employed in terrain too difficult for jeeps or other vehicles.

The children of military personnel put on a Christmas pageant at Fort Lewis in December 1950.

M. Sgt. Wilburn K. Ross, a Medal of Honor recipient, and M. Sgt. Arne Stenslie, popularly known as "Mr. Second Division," discuss the Korean War streamer on the colors of the 38th Infantry Regiment. Both men were distinguished veterans of that regiment.

A solemn high field mass was celebrated at the 91st Division Monument on May 10, 1953, to commemorate Mother's Day.

The 23rd Infantry Regiment baseball team poses for a group photograph at Fort Lewis prior to deploying to Korea.

The Indian head and star shoulder insignia of the 2nd Infantry Division has a long and historic association with Fort Lewis, Washington.

Seven

THE COLD WAR

Infantry and armor tactics are demonstrated on Fort Lewis around 1960. The M48-A2 "Patton" medium tank is armed with a flame thrower and is part of the 34th Armor. The infantrymen are from Company D, 1st Brigade, 8th Infantry Regiment.

The 4th Infantry Division arrived on Fort Lewis in 1956 and trained here until deployed to Vietnam in 1966. This photograph depicts infantrymen from the division admiring Mount Rainier.

A 105mm recoilless rifle, mounted on a jeep, fires at a target on Fort Lewis with Mount Rainier as a backdrop.

College students who were members of the Reserve Officers Training Corps (ROTC) frequently trained on Fort Lewis during the summer months. This photograph depicts a spirited member of the ROTC summer camp in training during the early 1960s.

ROTC cadets practice marksmanship on the rifle range at Fort Lewis, c. 1960. They are armed with M-1 rifles.

In 1954, World War II hero Audie Murphy filmed his autobiographical movie *To Hell and Back* on Fort Lewis and the Yakima Firing Center. Murphy was the most highly decorated soldier in American history and his epic movie recreated his World War II exploits. Here Audie Murphy poses with an American G.I. "extra" dressed in a German uniform.

During the filming of his movie, Audie Murphy was a respected and affable guest at several social functions on Fort Lewis. In this photograph, Audie poses with two admiring ladies. On his right is Mary Sink Meldrum, daughter of the Fort Lewis commander, Maj. Gen. Robert Sink. To Murphy's left is Tonnie Hawthorne, wife of Capt. Emile Hawthorne, aide-de-camp to Maj. Gen. Sink.

Mrs. Margaret Sink, wife of Major General Sink, talks with Audie Murphy during a reception on Fort Lewis. Murphy served with the Texas National Guard after the war and wears the shoulder insignia of the 36th Texas Division.

From 1917 to today, social functions form an important part of military life on Fort Lewis. This photograph dates from March 6, 1954 and depicts a reception line for Brig. Gen. Charles Swartz, new Commanding General for the 44th Infantry Division Artillery. Pictured, from left to right, are Mrs. R. Prather, Brig. Gen. R. Prather, Mrs. Isabelle Swartz, Brig. Gen. Swartz, Mrs. Margaret Sink, and Maj. Gen. Sink, Commanding General of the 44th Infantry Division.

The Army is a very multi-cultural society. This photograph depicts a Japanese suki-yaki dinner hosted by Asian wives on Fort Lewis. The dinner was prepared by the Japanese women to show appreciation for English classes conducted for them by "The Women of the Chapel." The dinner took place at the Religious Education Center on Fort Lewis on June 14, 1960.

Scouting has been an important part of life on Fort Lewis through the years. This 1961 photograph depicts a Cub Scout troop posing on an M48 tank with their den mother.

The Infantryman statue was dedicated on July 3, 1964, to honor the soldiers of the 4th Infantry Division. The statue was designed and built by SPEC. 4 Juan J. Guerrero. He designed the figure to represent all infantrymen assigned to the division. Even though the statue is constructed of resin and fiberglass, the Infantryman has come to be known as "Iron Mike." Originally the statue was located by the Nelson Recreation Center, but was moved to a more visible location, near the Main Gate, in 1992.

During a training exercise conducted in February 1960, men of Company E, 2nd Battle Group, 39th Infantry rush ashore at Solo Point, Fort Lewis. The ship is a LVTP 5, which belonged to the 560th Engineer Amphibious Equipment Company.

On November 25, 1963, a memorial service was held on Fort Lewis for the recently slain president, John F. Kennedy. This photograph depicts part of the solemn ceremony.

Fort Lewis officers and their families gather in front of the 91st Division Monument during the ceremony to honor President Kennedy.

Eight

THE VIETNAM WAR

An aerial view of the mock Vietnamese village built in the training area of Fort Lewis.

During his basic infantry training in 1970, Pvt. William A. Frank, from Chicago, fires his M-16 rifle on a Fort Lewis rifle range.

Pvt. James L. Hagan, from Yreka, California, throws a hand grenade before advancing on the Close Combat Course on Fort Lewis in May 1967.

Soldiers of the 3rd Battalion, 12th Infantry, 4th Infantry Division, participate in seize and search exercises at Fort Lewis in May 1966. The soldier on the left is Pvt. Gerald Hickey from Brooklyn, New York, and the soldier on the right is Pvt. Bobby D. Hatcher from Bristol, Wisconsin. The 4th Infantry Division deployed to Vietnam later in 1966.

Here is a view of the Vietnamese Village at Fort Lewis. Tens of thousands of soldiers trained here during the war in Southeast Asia. Although the climate of Fort Lewis was not comparable to Vietnam, the village did offer an opportunity to practice tactics employed in Vietnam.

Pfc. Darell Menke, from Peoria, Illinois, is "ambushed" by a G.I. dressed as a Viet Cong guerilla during training at the Vietnamese Village. The photograph was taken on May 5, 1967.

Pvt. Jack Bennett from Marion, Indiana, and Dean Redmond of Cedar Rapids, Iowa, man a M60 machine gun during field training at Fort Lewis. Both soldiers were assigned to Company C, 2nd Battalion, 3rd Basic Training Brigade in May 1970.

This is a sign familiar to tens of thousands of soldiers who trained at Fort Lewis during the Vietnam War period.

In September 1967, the veterans of the 91st Division returned to Fort Lewis to commemorate the 50th anniversary of their arrival at Camp Lewis in September 1917. The former doughboys had a grand time visiting the post, and the soldiers of Fort Lewis, who were training for the war in Vietnam, welcomed the veterans with open arms. This photograph was taken on September 15, 1967, and depicts Pioneer Club Hostess Mrs. Carol Geidel as she attempts to serve coffee to the veterans. On the left is Jack Price from Tacoma, veteran of the 361st Ambulance Company. Adjusting the World War I helmet is Stanley Potts, from Big Fork, Montana. To the right is Frank W. Read of Spokane. All were veterans of Company C, 362nd Infantry, 91st Division.

During the 50th Reunion of the 91st Division, the 400 veterans attending were treated to displays and demonstrations of modern Army weapons and equipment. Here, Leland Struble of Port Angeles, Washington, discusses the changes in army rifles with Sgt. Maj. Robert B. Clement (left), holding a World War I Springfield rifle, and Col. Robert W. Jamison, who demonstrates the new M16 rifle. Both soldiers were assigned to the Basic Rifle Marksmanship Committee Group.

Sgt. Maj. Robert B. Clement performs a tune on the bagpipes at a reception for the World War I veterans of the 91st Division at the Top Five NCO Club on Fort Lewis. The reception was held on September 14, 1967.

A future veteran is recognized on November 28, 1969. Pvt. Jimmie Herd of Tacoma was singled out as the 150,000th Basic Combat Training trainee at Fort Lewis. Brig. Gen. Thomas M. Tarpley, Deputy Commanding General of the U.S. Army Training Center Infantry and Fort Lewis, presents Pvt. Herd with a plaque and an engraved watch. The private trained with Company A, 4th Battalion, 1st Basic Training Brigade.

On July 10, 1969 a parade was held in Seattle to welcome home members of the 9th Infantry Division from service in Vietnam. The 9th Infantry Division saw heavy combat in Southeast Asia, particularly in the Mekong Delta area. Among the dignitaries on the reviewing stand was Secretary of the Army Stanley R. Resor, who is dressed in a belted trench coat. The soldier in combat dress is Staff Sgt. Harold Blye from Myrtle Beach, South Carolina. He was the recipient of two Silver Star medals for gallantry in combat in Vietnam. To his left is the reigning Seafair Queen, Miss Karen Johnson.

Nine

THE "OLD RELIABLES"

Brig. Gen. William B. Fulton welcomes the troops of the 3rd Battalion, 60th Infantry, 2nd Brigade, 9th Infantry Division, home from Vietnam in July 1969. The enlisted men of the "Old Reliables" look happy to be back at Fort Lewis.

On April 21, 1972, Fort Lewis was designated Headquarters, 9th Infantry Division and Fort Lewis. A gala reactivation ceremony was held on May 26, 1972 at Gray Army airfield on Fort Lewis. Army Chief of Staff William C. Westmoreland unfurled the 9th Infantry Division colors and presented them to Maj. Gen. William B. Fulton. Here, a division sergeant major assists Gen. Westmoreland in uncasing the colors of the 9th Infantry Division.

With the activation of the 9th Infantry Division, many army families came to live on Fort Lewis. Maj. James Knight, his wife Judy, and his three sons, Jeff, John, and Jim, represent the great families who have made their home on Fort Lewis through the years. All three Knight children grew up to serve as army officers, with two attending the military academy at West Point. This family portrait dates from 1975.

During the years that the 9th Infantry Division served at Fort Lewis, training for future conflicts continued around the clock, throughout the year. In this photograph a soldier is "rescued" by a UH1-V Medivac helicopter. The advances made in evacuating and caring for wounded and injured soldiers since the Korean War are nothing short of miraculous.

An M198, 105mm artillery piece is airlifted by a CH47 "Chinook" helicopter during training exercises on Fort Lewis in the 1980s. The guns of the 9th Division's artillery units could often be heard "booming" far into the night.

In 1980, Fort Lewis and the 9th Infantry Division were selected to host the High Technology Test Bed (HTTB). Through the use of advanced technology, the army hoped to create a rapid deployment force that could fight effectively, anywhere in the world, on short notice. The 9th Infantry Division was designated "Motorized" and they began to experiment with all types of new vehicles, weapons, and equipment. One of the most popular vehicles was the Fast Attack Vehicle (FAV). Based on a dune buggy, with a modified Volkswagen engine, the FAV was armed with all types of weapons from machine guns to rocket launchers. In 1983, the HTTB became the Army Development and Employment Agency (ADEA).

All was not work and training for the soldiers of Fort Lewis. In this photograph, an Army M151 jeep has been modified to serve as an appropriate vehicle for Santa Claus and his helpers.

Members of the Women's Army Corps played a major role in the history of Fort Lewis. On May 12, 1972 the 30th anniversary of the founding of the Corps was commemorated at a retreat ceremony on Fort Lewis. Staff Sergeant Diane L. Kappesser carries the flag down the path leading from the flagpole in front of the Post Headquarters.

During the late 1980s the 9th Infantry Division (Motorized) had a number of unique missions. One of them was to send soldiers to serve as part of the U.N. Peacekeeping Force in the Sinai. In this photograph, Maj. Gen. John Shalikashvili, Commanding General of the 9th Infantry Division (Motorized), visits with division troops serving a tour in Egypt. Usually, tours lasted approximately six months.

In spite of all the high technology training on Fort Lewis during the 1980s, basic marksmanship training continued to be an important part of the program. These soldiers fire their M16 rifles on a firing range on Fort Lewis. They are with the 60th Infantry Regiment, 9th Infantry Division.

During the hot, dry summer of 1988, the soldiers of the 9th Infantry Division (Motorized) were given a new mission: fighting forest fires in Yellowstone National Park. After receiving training from professional "fire jumpers," the soldiers were sent to the fire line where their discipline and hard work helped to save thousands of acres of national forest.

The forces of other friendly nations frequently trained at Fort Lewis. The band of the British Royal Parachute Regiment parades on Fort Lewis during the 1980s. The bands of the various foreign units usually made a good will effort to perform for appreciative American audiences.

In spite of new missions, "traditional" training continued at Fort Lewis as it has since 1917. In July 1975, SPEC. 4 Barbara Lowell of the Fort Lewis Women's Army Corps Company repels down a rope during "Adventure Training" at Huckleberry Creek Training Camp.

Not all trainees on Fort Lewis are human. The Fort Lewis Military Police regularly employ well-trained dogs to guard strategic locations, as well as to search for explosives, drugs, and other contraband. The dogs and their handlers are an impressive team and often demonstrate their skills to students and visiting dignitaries.

Another fabled and colorful unit that trained on Fort Lewis in 1984 were the 1st Battalion, 7th Duke of Edinburgh's Own Gurkha Rifles. The Gurkhas were known to be tough and resourceful fighters and also had a wonderful pipe band.

The 2nd Battalion (Ranger), 75th Infantry was activated at Fort Lewis on October 1, 1974. This battalion traces its lineage back to "Merrill's Marauders" who fought in Burma in World War II. The Army Rangers have earned the reputation as being among of the greatest fighting men in the world. However, in spite of their fighting skills, many of the Rangers are family men and outstanding members of the Fort Lewis community. This 1975 photograph depicts Army Ranger, Spc. C.R. Martin and his wife.

When the First Special Forces Group was activated at Fort Lewis on September 4, 1984, the post now had two elite units. Both the Rangers and the Green Berets maintain a standard of readiness and excellence in training that is unsurpassed in the army. Here a unit "patrols" a road in the Fort Lewis training area.

Ten

TRADITION MEETS TRANSFORMATION

Three great American soldiers were brought together for the I Corps Change of Command Ceremony on August 3, 1989: Gen. Colin Powell, Commanding General of U.S. Army Forces Command; Lt. Gen. Calvin A.H. Waller, incoming Commanding General of I Corps and Fort Lewis; and Lt. Gen. William H. Harrison, outgoing I Corps and Fort Lewis Commanding General. During Operation Desert Storm, Lt. Gen. Waller was selected to serve as Deputy Commander of American Forces in the Persian Gulf, under Gen. H. Norman Schwarzkopf. Following the coalition victory, Lt. Gen. Waller returned to Fort Lewis. Shortly after retiring in 1992, Waller passed away. The soldier-processing center on Fort Lewis was named "Waller Hall" in his honor. Colin Powell is presently the U.S. Secretary of State and William Harrison is mayor of Lakewood, Washington.

Lt. Gen. H. Norman Schwarzkopf served as Commanding General of I Corps and Fort Lewis from June 1986 until July 1987. He enjoyed the Pacific Northwest because of its natural beauty and outdoor recreational opportunities. General Schwarzkopf went on to command all American forces in the Gulf War and become one of America's greatest military heroes of the 20th century.

During Operation Desert Shield and Desert Storm a number of Fort Lewis-based units served in the Persian Gulf. Here, a returning Fort Lewis soldier embraces his young daughter.

Madigan Army Medical Center has been an important part of Fort Lewis since World War II. This aerial view shows the sprawling Madigan Army Medical Center complex as it looked prior to the construction of the new facility.

In 1985 construction began on a new state of the art medical facility on Fort Lewis. Seven years later, in 1992, the new eight-story, 414-bed Madigan Army Medical Center was officially opened. Because of incremental funding, the total cost of construction was $280 million—this was $95 million less than originally projected. Today, Madigan Army Medical Center is the busiest medical facility in the state of Washington and provides advanced medical care to active duty military personnel as well as the retired military community.

In 1999 work began to transform two infantry brigades at Fort Lewis into new vehicle mounted infantry organizations with high tactical mobility and hard-hitting capabilities. The 3rd Brigade, 2nd Infantry Division and the 1st Brigade, 25th Infantry Division, based at Fort Lewis, were selected to spearhead this transformation. The Interim Brigade Combat Teams (IBCT) are equipped with the latest in military vehicles and weaponry and are trained in all types of operations and tactics. Of course, any military operation ultimately depends on the teamwork, training, and courage of the soldiers. Sgt. Paul Castro, Pvt. Bill Everidge, and Spc. Robert Wiley, members of Team A, 1st Squad, 2nd Platoon, Company C, 1st Battalion, 23rd Infantry Regiment practice moving as a team during urbanized terrain training exercises.

Over the last several years, a number of innovative vehicles were tested at Fort Lewis by the IBCTs. Presently, the Light Armored Vehicle (LAV), initially loaned to the Army by the Canadian military, has been selected for use by the teams. Here, infantrymen from Team B, 2nd Squad, 2nd Platoon, Company C, 1st Battalion, 23rd Infantry Regiment, take cover after leaving the safety of their LAV III during live fire exercises in October 2001.

As the world turns and the army changes, it is more important than ever to preserve the history and traditions of the U.S. Army. The Fort Lewis Military Museum was established in 1971 to "collect, preserve, and interpret the history of Fort Lewis and the units that served here." The museum has a large collection of uniforms, weapons, and equipment that is used to convey the history of the American soldier who trained at Fort Lewis. This photograph depicts a World War II scene, commemorating the service of the units that deployed to overseas service from Fort Lewis.

Members of the 91st "Wild West" Division serving in France during World War I are depicted in this exhibit at the Fort Lewis Military Museum. Fort Lewis has the only certified U.S. Army museum on the west coast of the U.S. The museum's collection of Fort Lewis memorabilia is one of the finest in the country.

THE RED SHIELD INN
BUILT 1918-1919
HAS BEEN PLACED ON THE
NATIONAL REGISTER
OF HISTORIC PLACES
BY THE UNITED STATES
DEPARTMENT OF THE INTERIOR
PLAQUE DONATED BY FORT LEWIS CHAPTER
SOCIETY OF THE DAUGHTERS OF THE UNITED STATES ARMY

In 1973, the Fort Lewis Museum moved into the old "Red Shield Inn." The Inn had served as a guesthouse and officer's quarters from World War I, until a new guest facility was opened in 1972. In 1979, the Red Shield Inn was selected for placement on the National Register of Historic Places by the U.S. Department of the Interior. This plaque was donated by the Fort Lewis Chapter of the Society of the Daughters of the United States Army.

The Fort Lewis Military Museum remains dedicated to preserving the history of the post and the Army. Thousands of soldiers receive heritage training at the museum each year and tens of thousands of visitors learn about the history of the Army and Fort Lewis. The widow of Maj. Gen. David L. Stone, who supervised the construction of the post in 1917, donated the flagpole in front of the Fort Lewis Museum.

Although the Army is constantly evolving and changing, in order to remain on the cutting edge of military technology, this Fort Lewis bugler represents the tradition and timelessness of military duty.

The Main Gate, often called the Liberty Gate, remains a lasting symbol of Fort Lewis. Originally built in 1917, the gate was moved several miles north, to its present location when Interstate Highway 5 was built in 1956.

On August 4, 2001, Mr. William "Bill" Lake, a World War I veteran of the 91st Division, visited Fort Lewis. At 105 years of age, Mr. Lake is perhaps the oldest veteran to visit the post. He first came to Camp Lewis in October 1917 and, after training, left for France in June 1918 with the 362nd Infantry Regiment. Private Lake was assigned to the Machine Gun Company and was an ammunition carrier during the Meuse-Argonne Campaign in France. During combat, Private Lake had the heel of his boot shot off and several pieces of shrapnel tore his tunic. This visit marked the first time that Mr. Lake had been on post since 1918.

These are the soldiers of yesterday and today. During his visit to Fort Lewis, Mr. Bill Lake was hosted by present day members of the 4th Brigade, 91st Division (Training). Brig. Gen. Rodney Kobayashi accompanied Mr. Lake on a visit to the 91st Division Monument, the Fort Lewis Museum, and to a modern army mess hall. In spite of the years that separated World War I from the present, Mr. Lake and Brig. Gen. Kobayashi had a bond as soldiers that was unmistakable. As a banner in the Fort Lewis Museum proclaims: "Once a Soldier, always a Soldier."

ACKNOWLEDGMENTS

This book is the result of the kind assistance of many generous people and I would like to thank everyone who has supported both this project and the Fort Lewis Military Museum. If I missed anyone in the following list, please accept my apologies.

First of all, a thank you to my greatest supporters, the Board of Directors of the Friends of the Fort Lewis Military Museum: Col. (Ret) Ian Larson, Lt. Col. (Ret) Thomas Morgan, Mrs. Marion S. Ball, Col. (Ret) Isabelle J. Swartz, Sgt. Maj. (Ret) Clair Stairrett, Col. (Ret) Paul Knoop, Col. (Ret) Carroll Dickson, Col. (Ret) Patrick Powers, Col. (Ret) Jack Hertzog, and our President Emeritus, Brig. Gen. (Ret) Vasco J. Fenili. Other Friends of the Museum I would like to mention are: Maj. Gen. (Ret) John Hemphill, Lt. Gen. (Ret) William H. Harrison, Maj. Gen. (Ret) John Greenway, Mr. Orville Stout, Mrs. Beverly Bills, Mrs. Donnie Weeks, Mrs. Mary Osteriech, Mrs. Peggy Hemphill, Mrs. Robin Sink McClelland, Gen. (Ret) John Shalikashvili, and the late I Corps Historian, Mr. Joe Huddleston. Of course, I would also like to extend my appreciation to all our Museum Friends who support us throughout the year on so many projects.

Next, I extend my appreciation to the following friends and colleagues associated with Fort Lewis: Lt. Gen. and Mrs. James T. Hill, Maj. Gen. Roger L. Brautigan, Brig. Gen. William H. Brandenburg, Lt. Col. Joseph Shanney, Lt. Col. Robert Wrubleski, Mr. Walter Wilson, Mr. Thomas Meeks, Col. Luke S. Green, Cmd. Sgt. Maj. Paul M. Inman, Mr. John McGrath, Mr. Gregory Hagge, Ms. Synthia Santos, Mrs. Burndy Piccin, Mrs. Carol Pisano, Mrs. Marilyn Goodman, Mrs. Beatrice Ford, Master Sgt. Eddie White, Mr. James Kane, Mr. Robert Rosenburgh, Mr. James Solomon, Mr. James Symmonds, Mr. Joe Barrentine, Mrs. Barbara Sellers, Mr. Watson Evans, and Mr. Ken Mitchell.

Finally, last but not least, I would like to thank all the dedicated men and women who have served our nation on Fort Lewis from 1917 to the present.

THE FORT LEWIS MILITARY MUSEUM

FORT LEWIS, WASHINGTON